THE BRAGGY KING OF BABYLON

DANIEL 4:27-37 FOR CHILDREN

Written by Yvonne Holloway McCall
Illustrated by Jim Roberts

ARCH Books

© 1969 CONCORDIA PUBLISHING HOUSE, ST. LOUIS, MISSOURI
CONCORDIA PUBLISHING HOUSE LTD., LONDON, E. C. 1
MANUFACTURED IN THE UNITED STATES OF AMERICA
ISBN 0-570-06042-7

The king sat down on his throne with ease.
His tummy
sagged down
to the top
of his knees.

"I'm the glorious
Nebuchadnezzar,"roared he,

"The mightiest king
that the world will see."

Then he scowled as he peered from his lofty place
At a tall, dark man with a frowning face,

Who stepped from the shadows to face the throne
And spoke with a cool but warning tone,

"O King, you brag and swagger so,
But the kingdom is God's, not yours, you know.

"You may rule it now, but He'll take it away
If you keep on bragging and disobey.

"Give to the poor, who are hungry and weak."
But the king looked sullen and would not speak.

"I'll never give anything
away," thought he,
"For that would leave
a bit less for me."

Instead . . .

"Servants," he ordered,
"I want to invite
A thousand nobles to a
feast tonight!

"Have everything perfect
as perfect can be
As befitting the great
and powerful me!

"From my silver beads clean off every speck,
So they'll shine like moons around my neck.

"Make sure the goblets are shiny and bright.
They'll dazzle the eyes of my guests tonight.

"My kingdom is large, and I want to show
How great I am; the people should know."

He bragged and bragged,
"I have cattle and grain,
Elegant robes,
Nothing ragged or plain."

He never gave the beggars a bite to eat

Or sandals to wear on their bruised, bare feet.

But . . .

Later to himself he murmured aloud,
"I wonder if I'm getting much too proud."

He gazed at his great, walled city below,
Standing tall and proud in the sunset's glow.

So splendid it looked in the dusk of day,
His few humble thoughts soon faded away.

"Babylon, city majestic and grand —
I built it," he cried, "by my own mighty hand!"

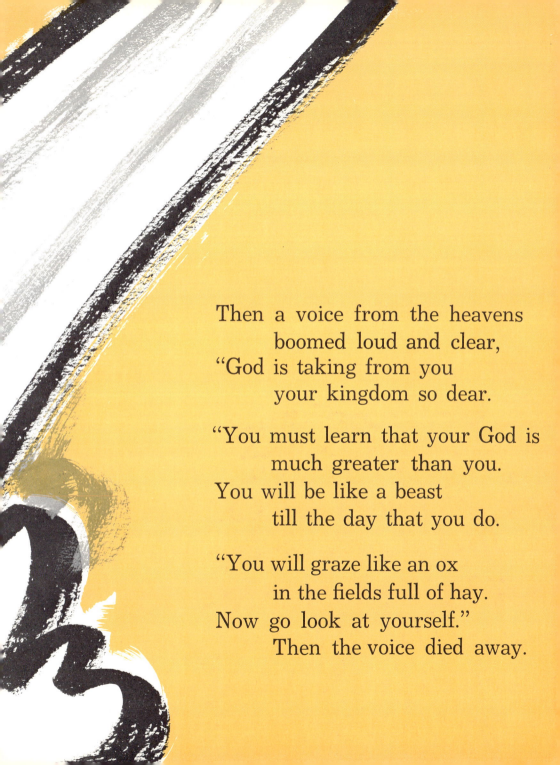

Then a voice from the heavens
   boomed loud and clear,
"God is taking from you
   your kingdom so dear.

"You must learn that your God is
   much greater than you.
You will be like a beast
   till the day that you do.

"You will graze like an ox
   in the fields full of hay.
Now go look at yourself."
   Then the voice died away.

The king then ran fast
till he came to his room,
He looked in the mirror
and saw his own doom —

All tangled and twisted,
the hair of the king
Was long as the feathers
of a big eagle's wing.

He wailed as he saw
he was shaggy and brown,
As he looked at himself
from the top on down.

He muttered, "Ridiculous!
Nothing is wrong —
Just a few more hairs,
and my nails are long.

"I don't look too bad!
I'm like a kingly beast.
I must get ready,
or I'll miss the feast."

As he crossed the room to the closet door,
His claws click-clicked on the marble floor.

He dressed in his best embroidered clothes
With the fringe that tickled his hairy toes.

He thought as he entered the dining hall,
"No one will notice the difference at all."

BUT . . .

He was met by a thousand shrieks at least.
The guests hurled goblets at the hairy beast.

The eyes of the king were filled with fear
When every guard reached for his spear.

He fled far away
to the fields to roam,
He cried and sobbed
in his strange,
new home.

In winter he shivered
from lack of heat.

In summer the dew
soothed his dry,
cracked feet.

As he woke one
morning at a
roaring sound,
He shook in his bed
on the lumpy ground.

Then he raced through the dew of a newborn day
From a stealthy young lion who was stalking
 his prey.

Then he hid and shouted to God in tears,
"I don't want to live like a beast for years.

"I thought I was mighty when I was king,
But You, O Lord, rule everything!"

So God changed him back to a king right then
And gave him his kingdom to rule again.

Thousands of great men gathered about
To welcome him back with a joyous shout.

And the bragging, swaggering days were gone
For the humble king of Babylon.

DEAR PARENTS:

Nebuchadnezzar ruled a great empire, but he overestimated his power. He called himself the mightiest king the world would ever see and thus assumed glory that belongs only to God.

Our story tells how God changed the heart of this "braggy king of Babylon." Nebuchadnezzar was "driven from among men and ate grass like an ox, and his body was wet with the dew of heaven till his hair grew as long as eagles' feathers, and his nails were like birds' claws" (Daniel 4:33). In his helpless condition the braggy king learned that he was only a man, completely dependent on God. When he came to his senses and praised God, his kingdom was restored to him.

Now the braggy king became the humble king who said, "Now I, Nebuchadnezzar, praise and extol and honor the King of heaven; for all His works are right and His ways are just; and those who walk in pride He is able to abase." (Daniel 4:37)

You can use this story to help your child recognize that boasting assumes power and honor that belongs to God. Help him feel that all strength and life come from God. Show him that God leads us to repent of our boasting and that He is ready to forgive because Jesus gave His life for us.

THE EDITOR